Where is it?

Bobbie Kalman

🌳 Crabtree Publishing Company
www.crabtreebooks.com

Created by Bobbie Kalman

For my cousin Matthew Brissenden
You have an amazing spirit. Shine on!

**Author and
Editor-in-Chief**
Bobbie Kalman

Editors
Reagan Miller
Robin Johnson

Photo research
Crystal Sikkens

Design
Bobbie Kalman
Katherine Kantor
Samantha Crabtree (cover)

Production coordinator
Katherine Kantor

Illustrations
© Crabtree Publishing Company: page 13

Photographs
© iStockphoto.com: front cover (mouse on cat),
    pages 4 (bottom), 6, 12, 13, 14, 16, 24 (top left and middle
    and bottom left)
© 2008 Jupiterimages Corporation: page 23 (top)
© ShutterStock.com: front cover (mouse in cup), pages 1,
    3, 4 (top left), 5, 7 (bottom), 9, 10, 11, 15 (bottom), 17,
    19 (B & C), 22, 23 (bottom), 24 (all except top left and
    middle and bottom left and right)
Other images by Corel, Digital Vision, and Photodisc

Library and Archives Canada Cataloguing in Publication

Kalman, Bobbie, 1947-
    Where is it? / Bobbie Kalman.

(Looking at nature)
Includes index.
ISBN 978-0-7787-3321-8 (bound).--ISBN 978-0-7787-3341-6 (pbk.)

    1. Orientation (Psychology)--Juvenile literature. 2. Geographical
perception--Juvenile literature. 3. Nature--Juvenile literature.
I. Title. II. Series: Looking at nature (St. Catharines, Ont.)

BF299.O7K34 2007   j508   C2007-904278-3

Library of Congress Cataloging-in-Publication Data

Kalman, Bobbie.
    Where is it? / Bobbie Kalman.
        p. cm. -- (Looking at nature)
    Includes index.
    ISBN-13: 978-0-7787-3321-8 (rlb)
    ISBN-10: 0-7787-3321-1 (rlb)
    ISBN-13: 978-0-7787-3341-6 (pb)
    ISBN-10: 0-7787-3341-6 (pb)
    1. Orientation (Psychology)--Juvenile literature. I. Title.
BF299.O7.K35 2008
153.7'52--dc22

                                    2007027239

Crabtree Publishing Company

www.crabtreebooks.com   1-800-387-7650

Published in Canada
Crabtree Publishing
616 Welland Ave.
St. Catharines, Ontario
L2M 5V6

Published in the United States
Crabtree Publishing
PMB16A
350 Fifth Ave., Suite 3308
New York, NY 10118

Published in the United Kingdom
Crabtree Publishing
White Cross Mills
High Town, Lancaster
LA1 4XS

Published in Australia
Crabtree Publishing
386 Mt. Alexander Rd.
Ascot Vale (Melbourne)
VIC 3032

Contents

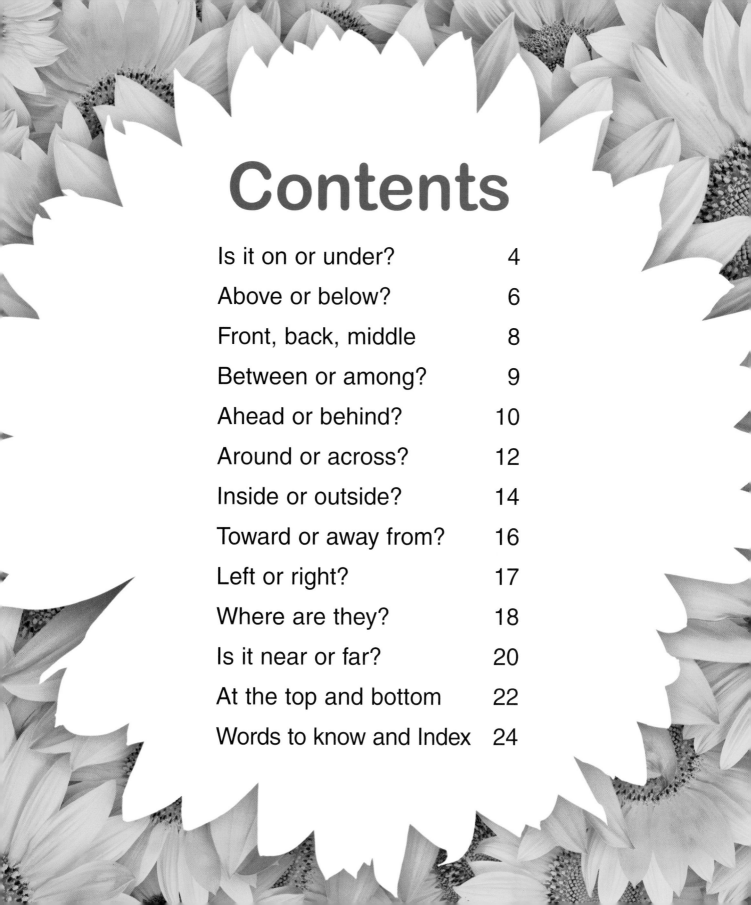

Is it on or under?

A cat is giving a mouse a ride. Is the cat **on** the mouse or is the cat **under** the mouse? Is the mouse on the cat or under the cat?

The alligator is under water.
You can see only its eye. Where
is the turtle? Is the turtle under
the alligator or on the alligator?

Above or below?

Where is the mouse now? The mouse is **below** the cat.

Where is the cat? The cat is **above** the mouse.

In the picture above, there is an ape. In the picture below, there is a groundhog. Which animal lives above the ground? Which animal lives below the ground? Where is the groundhog right now?

Front, back, middle

These three chimpanzees are sitting in a row. Which chimpanzee is in **front**? Which one is at the **back**? Where is the chimp in the **middle**? The middle chimp is **between** the other two chimps.

Between or among?

The cat above is hiding
among some flowers.
Among means between
more than two things. There
are more than two flowers.

Ahead or behind?

The elephants below are walking in a river.

One elephant is **ahead** of the other elephants.

How many elephants are **behind** it? Is the last elephant a mother elephant or a baby elephant?

How many baby elephants are walking in the river? Which baby elephant is ahead of the other baby elephants? Which baby elephant is behind the other baby elephants?

Around or across?

These rats are drinking from a bowl of milk.

The rats are **around** the edge of the bowl.

This lion is walking **across** a field. The lion is not walking around it. Walk across your schoolyard. Then walk around it. Which way took you longer?

around   across

Inside or outside?

One prairie dog is **inside** a hole. Another prairie dog is **outside** the hole. The hole is very deep. How will the prairie dog inside the hole get out of the hole?

14

This big fish is a grouper. Its mouth is **open**. There is a little gobi fish inside it. The gobi is cleaning the grouper's mouth. When the gobi is finished cleaning, it will swim out. The gobi will be outside the grouper's mouth. The grouper will then **close** its mouth.

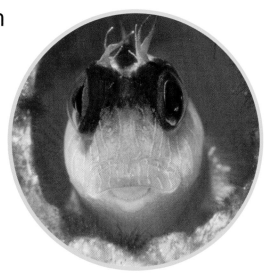

gobi

grouper

Toward or away from?

This mother hippo and her baby are by a river. The baby is walking **toward** the water. The mother is walking **away from** the water. Which hippo do you think is thirsty? Why do you think so?

Left or right?

Is the dog on the **left** or the **right** side of the boys in this picture? You are correct if you said the right side. Now pretend that you are the boy next to the dog. Is the dog on your right or your left side?

Where are they?

Sometimes animals hide, and it is hard to see them. Why do you think animals hide? Animals hide because they do not want other animals to find and eat them.

These tiny ocean animals have the same colors and spots as the places where they live. It is hard to see them.

All these animals are hiding.
Look at the pictures to answer
the questions below.

1. Which animal is hiding among some things?
2. Which animal is inside something?
3. Which is under something?
4. Which is hiding high above the ground?

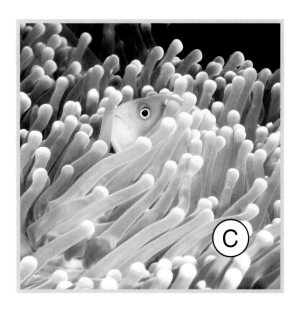

C

D

A

B

Answers:
1. C 2. D 3. A 4. B

19

Is it near or far?

Is this bear **far** from the tree or **near** the tree? The bear is near the tree. The bear is right **beside** the tree.

forest

field

river

There is a river, a field, and a forest in this picture. The bison is standing in the river. Is the bison beside the field or beside the forest? Is the bison near or far from the forest?

At the top and bottom

The **North Pole** is at the **top** of the Earth.

The **South Pole** is at the **bottom** of the Earth.

At the middle of the Earth is the **equator**.

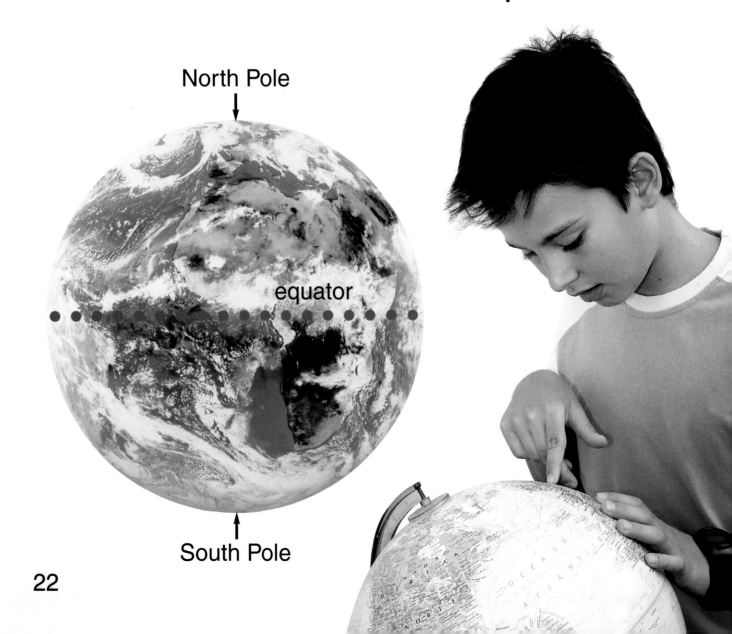

North Pole

equator

South Pole

The North Pole is a very cold place with snow
and ice. Polar bears live at the North Pole.

polar
bears

The South Pole is also very cold. It has a lot of snow
and ice, too. Penguins live at the South Pole.

penguin

monkey

It is very hot near the equator.
This monkey lives near the equator.

Words to know and Index

above
pages 6,
7, 9, 19

below
pages 6,
7, 10

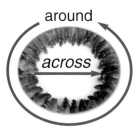

around

across

across, around
pages 12, 13

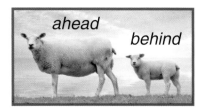

ahead

behind

ahead, behind
pages 10, 11

among
pages 9, 19

inside
pages 14, 15, 19

on
pages 4, 5

Other index words

away from, **toward**
page 16
back, front page 8
beside, far, near
pages 20, 21
between pages 8, 9
bottom, top page 22
left, right page 17
middle page 8

outside

outside
pages 14, 15

under
pages 4, 5, 19

Printed in the U.S.A.